·THE CAB[...]
PRINCESS

The little princess lived in a palace
with her two older sisters
and her father, the king.

She wore a high, gold crown
on top of her long, black hair.
Her dresses were stitched with gold
and jewels and peacock feathers.

But the princess wasn't happy.
Everyone who met her said
she was the unhappiest, grumpiest princess
they'd ever seen.

3

One day, the king called his three daughters.
"I'm giving you each a job to do.
The one who does her job best
will turn this kingdom into a queendom.
She will have my crown and my throne."

Then the king said,
"You, my first daughter,
you will go out and fight dragons.
You, my second daughter,
you will go out and hunt for treasure.
And you, my third daughter, you will look after
the palace vegetable garden."

The little princess was so upset
that she lay on the floor
and kicked and screamed.
"I want to fight dragons!
I want to find treasure!"

"There are plenty of dragons
and treasures in the vegetable garden,"
said her father.

The first princess got on her horse
and rode away to fight dragons.
The second princess got on her horse
and rode away to find treasure.
The third princess
went stamp, stamp, stamp,
into the garden.

A thrush in an apple tree
called to the little princess.
"There are plenty of dragons
to fight in this garden.
There is plenty of treasure, too.
Do your work well,
and you will discover
great riches."

The princess yelled
at the bird,
"What do you know,
big beak?"

But at the same time, the princess wondered
what treasure was hidden in the garden.
She stopped screaming
and began to pull out weeds.

Every day, the little princess worked
among the rows of vegetables.
She dug potatoes and tied up tomatoes.
She thinned carrots and picked beans.

She yelled at the thrush.
"Hey, big beak bird, you told me lies!"

"Keep on working," said the thrush.
"Just keep on working."

Before long, the palace vegetable garden
looked very neat.

The vegetables were at their best
when along came a cloud
of white butterflies.
They laid their eggs
on the cabbages.
The eggs became caterpillars
which ate the cabbage leaves.

"What will I do?" cried the princess.
"My beautiful cabbages look like old rags!"

"I think I can help you," said the thrush.
"But first, you must give me
your high, gold crown
and your long, black hair.
I need them to make a nest for my babies."

"Take them!" said the princess.

11

The little princess
put her crown
in the apple tree.
Snip, snip, snip.
The thrush cut off
her long, black hair
and made a nest
inside the crown.

Before long, the thrush
was back in the garden,
hopping from cabbage to cabbage
and eating all the caterpillars.

The little princess shook her head
and laughed her first laugh.
"My head feels so light
without that heavy
crown and hair!"

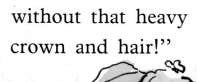

12

The caterpillars had gone,
but now the crows came to eat the corn.

"Please tell me what I should do,"
the princess begged the thrush.

"You must make a scarecrow
to scare the crows away,"
said the wise thrush.
"You'll need to use your dress
for the scarecrow."

The scarecrow kept the crows away
from the ripening corn.
All the vegetables grew strong and tall
in the sun.
And so did the princess.
Free from her heavy crown, hair, and dress,
she skipped about the garden,
whistling the songs
the thrush family taught her.

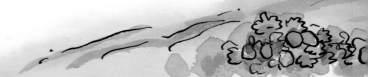

One afternoon, some visitors
came to the garden.
It was the king and the
two other princesses.
The king couldn't see his daughter,
but there among the lettuce plants
was a happy little boy,
singing like a bird.

"Tell me, my cheerful lad,"
said the king,
"where can we find the princess?"

"Father! I am the princess!"
laughed his daughter.
"I haven't seen any dragons
and not a scrap of treasure,
but I love working here."

"Dragons come in all shapes and sizes,"
said the king.
"They can be caterpillars or crows.
They can be dragons of unhappiness
or dragons of selfishness.
I think you've been fighting
a lot of dragons,
and you've won all your battles."

"What about treasure?" asked the princess.

"Treasure comes in all shapes and sizes, too,"
the king replied.
"You've found the treasure of hard work;
the treasure of sun, wind, and rain;
the treasure of a good friend.
Best of all,
you've found the treasure of happiness.
I'm going to make *you*
queen of this land."

19

The princess laughed.
"No thanks, Father," she said.
"I've found another treasure, too.
It's called freedom.
I never want to wear a heavy crown
or live in a stuffy, old palace again."

Then the other two princesses
cried to their father,
"We want to live in the garden, too!"

The king nodded.
"So do I," he admitted.

The king decided that his country
was big enough to look after itself.
He turned the palace into a museum,
and all the family
moved into the garden shed,
where they sold vegetables for a living.

Every morning,
the family of thrushes in the apple tree
sang about the treasures
of sun and wind and rain,
the treasure of good friends,
and the treasure of green, growing things.
The royal family called it their freedom song
and lived happily ever after.